J
796.6
WOO
Wood, Tim
Mountain biking

$10.40

DATE DUE			
DE 26 '89	JY 17'00		
AG 20 '91			
OC 18 '93			
OCT 16 '95			
AU 06 97			
NV 07 97			
NV 28 98			
AR 02 98			
JL 15 98			
AP 13 '00			
JA 17 '00			
JY 05 02			

MY SPORT
MOUNTAIN BIKING

Tim Wood

Photographs: Chris Fairclough

Franklin Watts

London • New York • Sydney • Toronto

© 1989 Franklin Watts

Franklin Watts
387 Park Avenue South
New York
NY 10016

Phototypeset by Lineage, Watford
Printed in Italy
Designed by: K and Co

ISBN: 0-531-10829-5
Library of Congress No: 89-50202

Illustrations: Simon Roulestone

The publishers, author and photographer would
like to thank Sean Bolland and the London
Mountain Bike Club for their help and
cooperation in the production of this book.

The photographs on pages 28 and 29 were
supplied by Maximum Exposure Ltd.

The mountain biker featured in this book is Sean Bolland. Sean is sixteen and still attends school. He has always enjoyed running and took up orienteering at the age of seven. He has won many orienteering championships and has twice been the British National orienteering champion for his age group. Sean took up mountain biking three years ago when he had a chance to ride a bike owned by a family friend. Sean entered the National Championships in 1987 but failed to finish in the final when his front fork broke. He became British Junior Champion in 1988. Sean still cannot decide which of his two sports he likes best.

I am a mountain biker. Tomorrow I am going to Snowdonia to practice, so I check my bike. I find I have a puncture. I use tire levers to loosen the tire and then remove the inner tube.

I spread rubber cement evenly around the puncture in the inner tube.

I put a special rubber patch over the hole
and hold it tightly until the cement dries.

After the cement has dried, I slip the inner tube back into the tire casing. I make sure that the tire does not pinch the inner tube, as this might cause another puncture. Then I put the wheel back between the forks.

Once I have bolted the wheel in place, I pump up the tire. I have to do my own repairs during a race, so I usually carry two spare inner tubes. It is quicker to put on a new tube than it is to repair a puncture.

I adjust the rear gear changer. My bike has six rear gears and three front ones, giving a total of eighteen gears altogether. Some of them are very low to help the bike go up steep slopes.

9

The front cantilever brakes are easy to
check. The brake wires unclip and the brake
block swings out.

10

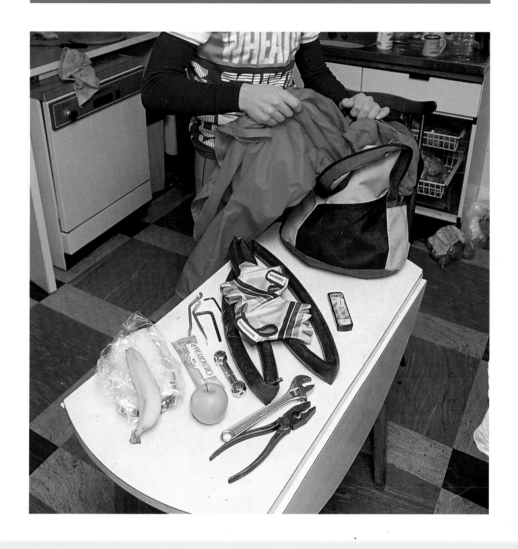

Once I have checked the bike thoroughly, I go inside and pack my haversack. I take a few tools in case I need to repair the bike and a rain coat in case it rains. I also pack a lunch as I will be out all day.

Early next morning, I cycle to the station and
load my bike onto the train. I live in a
very flat area, so I have to travel some
distance to find steep mountains.

About an hour later, I arrive at a station in Wales. I check the map to find the tracks I will use.

More about mountain biking

My mountain bike is a Bromwich Custom and was specially made for me. It has a hand-made frame and aluminum alloy wheels. The manufacturer gave it to me. He hopes that if I do well, other people will want to buy his bikes. The bike has no extras. Even the mudguards have been stripped off to reduce the weight. It has three front gear wheels. The outer ones are circular but the center one is elliptical to give extra power for climbing hills.

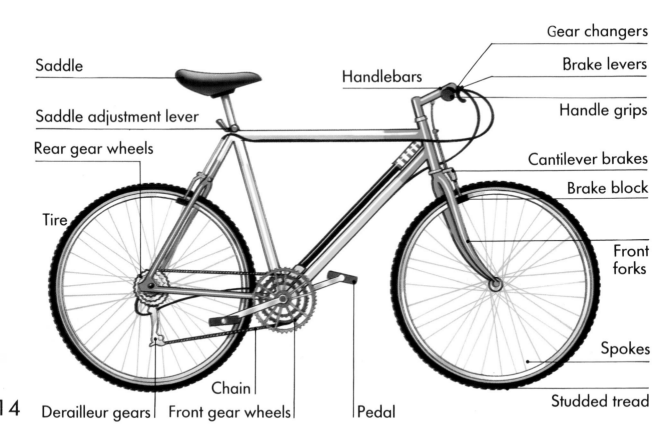

Saddle

Saddle adjustment lever

Rear gear wheels

Tire

Gear changers

Brake levers

Handlebars

Handle grips

Cantilever brakes

Brake block

Front forks

Spokes

Studded tread

14   Derailleur gears   Front gear wheels   Chain   Pedal

The rider's view

The gear shifts are "indexed." The right one selects the six rear gears and the left one selects the three front gears. The handlebars are made of a strong but light steel alloy. The front brakes are wire controlled cantilevers. Some mountain bikes have more powerful brakes, but these are easy to repair and adjust. The tires have studded treads to improve grip. My tires are a little narrower than those on a normal mountain bike. This gives my bike extra speed but makes it harder to control.

15

I leave the road as soon as I can and ride on the tracks.

Mountain biking is not only good exercise, it also takes you to some beautiful places. I have to ride cautiously across the bridge as the timbers are very slippery.

Mountain biking is becoming very popular.
I soon meet some other bikers and we talk about
the best tracks to use.

After about an hour's ride, I reach high ground above the tree line. In some places, the mountain is too steep for riding so I carry my bike and run up the slope as fast as I can.

19

Near the top, I stop to enjoy the spectacular view. I am feeling hungry and a bit tired so I decide it's time for a rest.

As soon as I stop moving, I realize that the wind is very cold so I put on my windbreaker. It will keep me from cooling down too much while I have my lunch.

The rocks shelter me from the wind while I eat and rest.

I put on my special cycling gloves. My hands don't move much while I am cycling, so they get quite cold. The gloves have rubber strips on the fingers which help me to grip the handlebars firmly.

After lunch, I decide to go on. When going up hill, I use less energy if I sit down to ride. However, I also need to put weight on the back wheel to make it grip, so I raise my saddle to help me ride more efficiently.

Riding over rocky ground is uncomfortable so I stand up on the pedals. I pick my way carefully. Being able to choose the best route over bad ground can make the difference between winning and losing a race.

Going down this steep slope, I sit further back to move my weight over the rear wheel. I lower my saddle before making the descent. This gives me better control over the bike.

The bike will go almost anywhere, even
through a bog! Unfortunately, my front wheel
catches in a hidden ditch and I fall off.
I am wet and tired. It is time to go home.

Here I am at the National Mountain Bike Championships. I am a junior so I start at the back of the field, behind the seniors.

During the race, I manage to overtake most of the seniors and finish among the first twenty riders. I was first in my own class and so became Junior British Champion. The practice on the mountain certainly paid off!

Facts about mountain biking

Mountain biking began in the United States. The first mountain bikes were ordinary road bikes. They only had five gears, so the riders mostly pushed their bikes uphill and then enjoyed the bumpy ride down.

Mountain bikers soon wanted to ride uphill as well, so they began to add derailleur gears. These were similar to those used on racing bikes but with much lower ratios to help the rider go up steep hills.

The first mountain bikes were long. This made them more stable going downhill but slower to ride uphill. Gradually, as frame design improved, bikes became shorter. This made them quicker and easier to maneuver round obstacles. The metal used for the frames changed too. Experiments with lighter, stronger materials like chromium and molybdenum steel (Cro-Mo), aluminum, carbon fiber and kevlar have made the bikes much tougher and lighter, although they also became very expensive.

Gear changing has been made easier with the introduction of indexed gears. Indexed gears make gear changing much faster and more accurate. Some mountain bike producers are working on electronic gearshifts that will allow the rider to change gear while pedaling at full speed.

One of the toughest mountain bike races must be the Paris to Dakar. Riders start at the Eiffel Tower and ride 4,000 miles across Africa. They climb over the Atlas Mountains in bitter cold and then cross the Sahara Desert in blazing heat.

GLOSSARY

Alloy
A mixture of metals.

Brake blocks
Rubber blocks that grip the wheel rim when the brakes are applied and slow the bike.

Cantilever brakes
Brakes that use hinged levers to push the brake blocks onto the wheel rim to produce powerful and smooth braking.

Carbon fiber
A light but very strong plastic.

Cro-Mo
Chromium-molybdenum steel alloy.

Derailleur gears
A system of bike gears that works by moving the bicycle chain from one gear wheel to another.

Gears
A set of cog-wheels over which the bike chain passes, by which the power of the pedals is transmitted to the wheels.

Indexed gears
Gears that allow the rider to change gear quickly and accurately by moving the shift lever one slot up or down.

Orienteering
A special form of cross-country running race. The runners have to find their way across country using maps and compasses.

Rubber cement
Glue used for repairing punctures.

Tire lever
Flat metal rod used for levering a tire off the wheel rim.

Index